The Lone Man
Near the Window

The Lone Man Near the Window

"Jharka Pakhara Ekala Manisha"
Original work in Odia language

Dr. Bibhudatta Nayak

English Rendition:
Madhumita Dash

BLACK EAGLE BOOKS
Dublin, USA | Bhubaneswar, India

 Black Eagle Books
USA address:
7464 Wisdom Lane
Dublin, OH 43016

India address:
E/312, Trident Galaxy, Kalinga Nagar,
Bhubaneswar-751003, Odisha, India

E-mail: info@blackeaglebooks.org
Website: www.blackeaglebooks.org

First International Edition Published by
Black Eagle Books, 2024

THE LONE MAN NEAR THE WINDOW
Original work in Odia Language "Jharka Pakhara Ekala Manisha"
Dr. Bibhudatta Nayak
English Rendition : **Madhumita Dash**

Original copyright © Dr. Bibhudatta Nayak
Translation copyright © Madhumita Dash

All rights reserved. No part of this publication may be reproduced, stored in a retrieval system, or transmitted, in any form or by any means, electronic, mechanical, photocopying, recording or otherwise without the prior permission of the publisher.

Cover design: **Trilochan Sahu**
Interior Design: Ezy's Publication

ISBN- 978-1-64560-524-9 (Paperback)
Library of Congress Control Number: 2024933422

Printed in the United States of America

Dedicated to :
My dear late father Sri Niranjan Dash
and
My father-in-law Sri Raghunath Mahapatra

The Prologue

"Success doesn't mean the absence of failures. It means the attainment of ultimate objectives. It means wining war not every battle." - Edwin C. Bliss

All art is at once like a surface or a symbol. And an artist goes beneath the surface and reads the symbols of life. An artist always aims to mirror the diversity of beauty, reality of the concealed thoughts, morality experiences and veneer of emotions before the readers or the spectators.

This book, The Lone Man Near The Window, is like an identity to the experiences of a keen family person in his/her lonesome moments. It is not only about the poet's life, lessons, thoughts rather an extension of you, me and all sensitive persons who in real face, feel and resemble such phases narrated in each individual poetries.

This piece of art can't be absorbed by a one go reading. Though it is adorned with very simple words yet has deep impacting topics orchestrated with word senses and harmony.

The concept and the purpose of the book can't be gulped down in a single reading. To understand the seamless process one has to live each and every philosophy coated in words. .

The original book by revered Poet Dr.Bibhudatta

Nayak is literally an experience manual which describes the tit bits of life tools. It enlists the ingredients and principles of life which make our lives sweet, sour, annoying, energetic, challenging, emotional, decisive, philosophical at times. Most of the experiences of daily chores in this mundane world have given an euphonious shape of distinct poetry in this book.

For years together while perusing a very casual and normal life reading to different literary pieces, doing households, imparting duties and responsibilities I suddenly woke up with a desire to challenge my ability of doing something I love beyond the comfort zone.

A very keen and sensitive reader like me might have risen to think beyond the book where s/he found active self involvement in each poem. A thorough minute reading deliberately ignited a sense in me to reincarnate this amazing work of art into another form.

The decision to translate this book was not undertaken in a fluke. But to assess the lost self ability and as a gesture of appreciation of a beautiful work of art. With the conviction to transcreate the whole book of fifty poems, I started exploring the other dimensions of my personality. Reading different works and writing my own experiences were in the base for which I am always in love with art and literature and its aesthetics. I put my sincere efforts to translate the book in English keeping the original essence and aesthetics intact.

During the process many shortcomings surprised me many times. Yet I could complete this journey of my own challenge and reached the goal on time by the grace of Lord Jagannath. .

My deepest thanks to respected Poet to believe in me and allow me to carry forward the project. His kind and humble guidance cannot be overlooked. My sincerest gratitude to my family and friends to cope and deal with my busy schedule while I was engrossed in my work. My loving thanks to Mr. Trilochan Sahu for the apt cover design. Lastly my humble thanks to the Publication House to publish my translated book.

Madhumita Dash

Bhubaneswar
16 January 2024

A Short Discourse

I used to keep on watching through my window an aged couple do walk slowly everyday in the park in front of my house. After completing their morning walk, they sit on the bench in the park for sometime, enjoy the warmth of the tender morning sunshine there, chit chat a bit with others who all come to roam in the park. After some days I notice, the old man comes alone and walks slowly keeping his head down. After the walk, he sits for a while alone on that same cement bench. Others come to the park as usual but he doesn't ever talk to anyone anymore. Only keeps looking at the sky silently.

The man is left behind alone.The one who is the closest to him and stayed with him for more than five decades, vowed to walk the whole life holding his hands, leaves for heavenly abode. His children, who learnt walking by holding his finger, also fly away to make their own nest with someone else. He is left behind all alone. This is perhaps the fact of life. Many a time we are left alone. We feel alone even in the crowd.

What else a lone man can do except staring at the sky !! The ambience beyond the window looks very festive. Whereas, this side of the window, there is a lost soldier in life's battle sitting all alone. Now he has no intent to win nor any regret of losing. He has no more desire to achieve nor there is any rage about not achieving anything. He doesn't greet light nor fears darkness anymore. This calm unmoving lone man near the window subconsciously goes on dreaming which is beyond his control !!

The lone man waits, searches for his own existence in his own illusory desired world, runs after the golden deer of temptation, unites the earth and the sky, gets hurt by the cactus flower, yet acts to be happy. Many questions arise in his mind. The lost man searches for truth in the void. Burns and exhausts in the lighthouse. Yet he is denied to cry or shed tears. This is Life !!

This book is an honest try to create a lively portrait of many dimensions of life by orchestrating and decking up words through the poems. I extend my sincere gratefulness to many, especially to Paschima Publication for bringing it out. Lastly, my gratitude for my dear friend Dr. Tarun Ojha for designing the beautiful cover page.

12.09.2022   **Bibhudatta Nayak**

CONTENTS

Waiting	15
The Felon	17
The Supreme Mother	19
Crust	21
The World I Look For	23
The Lone Man Near The Window	25
The Pinwheel Flower	27
You Are Near By...	29
Aflame	31
Annihilation	33
Power Cut	35
The Vanquished Time	37
The Cascading River	39
The Light House	41
The Incarcerated	43
No More Tears	45
The Voidness	47
In Search of Truth	49
Yes, I Am Alive!	51
A Loser	53
The Parched	55
The Lass from Different Agnate	56

The Sea	57
After Losing Something	59
An Illusory Deer	61
Bond	63
Winsomeness	64
Question Mark	65
Flower of Cactus	66
When you Left!!	67
Illusion	69
Gambling	70
Existence	71
Paper Boat	72
Forgetfulness	74
Beyond Expectations	76
The Touch	78
The River	80
From Earth to the Sky	81
Holi	83
Poet	84
The Flower	86
This is Life	88
Pretension	89
Happiness	90
Delusion	91
Mynah Soared High	93
Incomplete	95
Butterfly Doesn't Get Caught	97
The Painted Enthrallment	99

Waiting

Waiting is not painful all the time,
It brings satiety too
Sometimes, it confines the affinity to live
As if, to wait is the whole mainstay of life.

Am aware that you won't come
Still the wait goes on
From the mounts of Shikharchandii
I wait for the mist to obliterate
And to listen to the muffled bombilation of known traits.

The wait in the beachside
To recollect and reminisce
Of the dreams we saw together, and
The golden gleamy rays of twilight,
The wait is for you to stumble upon me
While you would try to go away from the waves
As the sudden curls and ridges advance towards your feet.

The wait is for the walls of the sandcastle to reach
To an ostensibly superficial height,
Which would help me build a roof on top of it
Where I could hide myself
To paint all my desires for you
Embracing, caressing and cuddling all my longings.

Now, the wait has become
Unabatingly yet habitual
Seemingly, to get something and owning has no charm inside,
To enjoy the wait is
Rather congenial and pleasurable
These days, time doesn't go by
Every day is exhausted with a long wait
As if there is no more
Objective of life.

●

The Felon

I am the felon
there is no account of
how many murders and loots I have committed!

I have secretly murdered many of my irresistible desire
Repeatedly strangulated all the aspirations
and buried them alive!

I have robbed the colours of all my dreams
Split as under all the sapphires and gems
I have eliminated them,
Suppressed brutally all the voices those rose against me
And busted the laughter that rose without my sanction!

I am a cruel felon
I have hurt the ones whom I loved the most.
I have confined the fairy
and her wings in a tenebrous place
I chopped her innocence into pieces!

When she helplessly writhes,
I cachinnated with satiety of fiendish desires
like a discounted soul,
I have cackled loud and shaken the land to the whole earth!
When I look back to the spectacular mansion
And the magnificent empire,

Once I have established in reference to the virility,
I found there is nothing left
Except some derelict walls,
Some relics and remnants of a forlorn dreary city
The birds I nurtured have flown away
leaving the seeds of pearls.

Now I am all alone
Worthless and stupefied,
An absolute felon!!

The Supreme Mother

Be with me always
In my enchantment
As well in resentment
In my attachment
And in detachment
In my conclusion
As well in my decision.

Be with me always
In my faith and breath
In my comfort and oath
In my deep sighs
In my enthusiasm and ardour
Be there in my dreariness and unwell
In my exertion and exuberance as well.

Be with me always
In my requirements
In my restraints
In deep petulance,
Be a part of my rise and fall
In invocation and immersion
In greetings as well.

Be with me always
In possibility and plausibility

In shaping up my feasibility
I wish you to be in my
Worship and in adoration
In distraction and in reprehension
In devout prayer and felicitation.

Be with me always
In all my directions
In the northeast
In southeast
In southwest
And in Northwest too.

In the zenith
In nidar as well
In east, west, right and left
In all my sides stand with me tall.

I shall continue to be with you forever
Just like a cranky child.
I will strive amongst
All the living entities
In light and anonymity
In auspicious as well in inauspicious days.
Till I get you,
I shall be seeking for the blessings and security of Annapurna
Shall continue to remain an obstinate
Till I find you.

Always with me you be there
Till my last breath
That is all, I insist and wish for.

The Crust

When faces any eye contact,
the invertebrate creature inside the conch
hides itself inside its shell !
Not known what sin it has done
But it has to carry the heavy crust
Wherever does it crawl!

There is no dearth of
Cruel insatiable flesh eaters on this earth,
To live, it is necessary to
Preserve life secretly in an unfathomable depth,
What is there to brood over?
She is imprisoned in the hands of the prince
Of her own dreams!

She has to carry the heavy crust all through!
To get an assent of the unwanted life.
Being aware of her short murky life alike the mist,
She has borne in darkness and will fade away in darkness...
The life will be finished beneath the crust.

Is there anything to call her own?
She has acquiesced the body, sweat, effort, modesty
She has minimized herself,
Even her hopes and aspirations with ease,
Set herself inside the dimension of the conch shell

She has spread her generous peerless pearly smile
Like the sun scatters its tender rays.

Whenever she comes out of the shell
Plays a lot, roams, and preys...
Draws lines on the sand bed of sea...
May be singing in her own language,
Even if she wants can't able
To welcome in on anyone's arrival
Can't open up to say anything...
Again she enters into the conch shell
And imprisons herself inside the narrow channel of darkness.

The outer world is completely different
From the dark valley inside the conch shell.
Creativeness is always soulful and emotional...
Still she couldn't write a fiction beyond the shell,
Even couldn't write a poem any day
Relating to the darkness she is confined
It couldn't complete the drawings of the mountain, fountain;
Trees near to the fountain, swing and cottage!
That invertebrate creature inside the conch shell
Never expected more than as much as she has already dwell!

●

The World I Look For

Many nights like this
I have waited for whole night,
Sitting in the balcony on my rocking chair
To see the sight of a shooting star
I have lots of wishes
And there are many things to ask for!!

I have to ask for
A calm, cool, dense, green,
Generous, authentic compliant world
Without any boundaries, any border!
I would seek for some oxygen,
To meet the hunger of
Stomach, body and only by exhalation.
To help to sprout healthy body and reflection!!

I want to ask for immense power
And potential from God,
The Pashupatastra
Endless arms and armaments
An inexhaustible quiver,
An open third eye
A strong willpower to dissolute all vile
And to establish virtue forever!

I waited for many nights with unflinching eyelids
Wanted and wished only for a shooting star,
But in the quietude of lonely night
An anxious cry of a bird was heard continually,
Don't know why that bird was crying
What was its problem?
Caste or religion!
Unemployment!
Reservation!
Hunger!
Victim of rape!!
But, the bird has neither any limitations
Nor any discrimination of religion
No rule affixed
Neither Constitution
Yet, why this pitiable lamentation!!

A dog keeps barking ceaselessly
Only within a very short distance!!
May be it was sensing something unusual...
Perhaps it becomes suffocated
With the stench of unfaithfulness.
As if sincerely pleading...
There is still time to get better to be human!!

May be the stars got aware
And thus didn't shoot at all!
But, I am mulishly unyielding
I shall wait till the epoch time
Shall ask for my desirable world till my last
I shall never quit!
I shall never quit!!

The Lone Man Near the Window

Don't know what the man was staring at
Sitting near the window!

Alone, on his own
Day after day
Months and years together
Towards the azure sky all alone he used to stare,
He used to count on fingers
All the pains the whole life he stored,
The lonely man near the window was dealing with the clouds!

With the beats of wings of the homecoming storks,
His grey eyelids quiver
Which used to be alike a dried up river before.
His eyes are fixed on the blue sky
And the blue sky reflects in his eyes...
Don't know,
For whom the lonely man is waiting for
Sitting near the window!

Even after the dusk
He sits imperturbable near the window,
Gazes at the sky
And is surprisingly nonchalant about the darkness and light
Rain, spring, summer, and winter night.
How would it matter even??

It's long since his Sun has set in the west
The sun doesn't wish to rise again...
His earth has no rotation,
Yet waits the lonely man
Whole night for the twilight to break open
Sitting near the window all alone!

Perhaps he used to plead the clouds
Was wishing for the final drop of decease
A little freedom from the state of living demise.
When vision, stomach, hearing, reflection, all get dulled,
Then the intensity of breath only remains stronger.
May be that is the intensity before extinguishing...
Probably it has been burning years together
And burning life before fading away...
And the lone man sitting near the window
Was looking for his share of death all alone!

He interrogates himself
Gives reason and replies on his own...
Makes mistakes and finds out the error by himself,
He rectifies his flaws else punishes himself...
Silently he suffers the punishment
Sitting near the window all alone
He loses himself quietly in the sonorous silence!

Perhaps a lone man has nothing called grief and misery in his life!!
Who is there to listen to his plight...?
Except some silence, little quietude
An open window,
Petal like clouds on the other side of the window...
Who is there other than these, to whom he would reveal his pain?
Sitting near the window all alone!

The Pinwheel Flower

The white pinwheels
Bloom in plenty
And fall on its own
No one cares about these flowers.

It has no shade
No beauty
Perhaps, this is the reason
It is not much adored and the loved one.

It is like the ipomoea carnea
Flourishes in ample anywhere
Anyone can pluck a handful of them
For its easy reachability and convenience
Thus it becomes nugatory and lacks adoration.

No one offered her a handful of soil ever
At no time watered with a tiny earthen saucer either
Not at any time nobody decorated their own garden
With these flowers
Rather it is always found near to the premises
And available to all on stretch of hands
They pluck it effortlessly and in bunches.

The pinwheel flowers must have some desires
To be embellished someday in the

Chignon of a beautiful lady
A wish that one would wrote verses
And a few words admiring her.

These days vaunting and barging
Are highly sought after
If you do not pomp and splendour
The busy world around
Which counts life as nothing but a bed of flowers
Do not get the reality ever.

The life of this pinwheel is identical
To the life of a simple
Innocent and ordinary human
Nobody bothers and either shows any compassion.

●

You Are Near By

I feel you are here nearby,
Somewhere around me
Sitting in the chapel to worship
And quietly holding the chanting rosary in hand.
As if you would say something
Or would call me with gestures of hand,
But waiting for the chant to end...
Don't know, all the time for all of us what you ask your God.

I feel you are around here somewhere in the yard...
And engrossed in making the colourful rangoli art,
Your whole winter morning passes
in doing rangoli one by one
You keep yourself busy in serving
the hundred and eight sets of prasad
In tiny pieces of banana leaves
You spend your entire time with your adored deities!

I feel as if you are somewhere around the next room...
Sitting with your face down immersed in a page of Purana,
As if you are writing musical canto and quartet in your contorted handwriting
And have filled all the old diaries that I gave
I feel as if you will come and ask me
now to copy those to my lap top.

I feel you are around here somewhere in the living room...
Sitting on the sofa and waiting for my homecoming from office
As soon as I enter the house
As if you would touch my head and ask
'Oh son! Was there a lot of work today?
Why you look so tired?'
Whenever I keep my head in your lap and lie down a little
All my weariness would vanish away within a while.

Don't know why
I always look leaner, skinny, and weary in your eyes
These days I really feel very exhausted,
Wherever you are,
Just touch my head and keep me blessed.

●

Aflame

I have lived and died inch by inch
A lot for myself,
If I can be the food for making someone else alive,
Then it would impart a great value in the life.

Many venomous reptiles conceal themselves for their preys.
Use their tails as baits,
Even knowingly or unknowingly
If someday
I reach anyone's premises,
What is the harm?
If one lives a few days more
Feeding on me,
Where lies the fault?
As its nature is to feed on others
If not me, some other would be its prey,
And be burnt by its ego!!

I got burned, that is true.
But the fuelwood burns too
Till it boils a pot of rice for others.
Water, air, rain, sky, darkness, light, sun, moon, the whole earth
Selflessly surrender and serve the mankind.
Let today be my turn, why to mind?

Let the self-conscious and the wicks of egotism
Be the flame of fire!
But for how many days?
Here the blaze and the inflammable;
Anything and everything is combustible.
To live is nothing but putting oneself on fire.

Annihilation

When I was busy and occupied in my own world
You appeared as a melodious amalgamation
Of symphonic dance and tunes,
Ignorantly opened the woven laths
in the wave of your melody.
Sometimes it was dissonant lacking harmony,
Some other time got carried away with
the tempo of the rhythm.
Sang the boatman's chants...
Don't know when did I step forward
With you to an unknown destination.

With the fragrance of your assurance
I sowed two seers of paddy seedlings
in the gravelled red clay bed
Where you grew imaginary crops
The whole field was filled with
The golden waves of linseed flower.
I was totally intoxicated with
The tipsy smile of the mahua wine,
The shadow of the aromatic plumeria was
Gathering fistful of attachment
And was drying my innocent sweaty body
As if the skirt of sari is fanning me.

That evening you gave me a flute
Wrapped in red velvety cloth, near the bur flower tree,
You taught me to attune and accord the flute
And learn ragas Todi Madhuvanti Hamsadhwani in a spree.
To stand in cross legs and to give a sidelong glance.
In spite of trying thousand times
Putting all my breath and effort
I could only play your name.

Now in my solitudinous moment
What kind of observation is this!
The river is there
The field is there
The bur flower tree is there
But there is no tune of flute.
My world is left void in darkness
Neither you are there, nor left any footprint.

●

Power Cut

Sometimes an unanticipated uncalled gust of darkness
Invades the periphery of our lives,
while many things appear clear and easy
It shakes the vigour, fortitude, trust, rumination and the soul.

Sometimes an unanticipated gust of darkness....
is perhaps like the forecast of a storm,
these are unspecified and
Inexplicit storms like an unsatisfied soul.
Even after making things upside down a lot
Smile with sheer peace and takes pleasure in hurting others.

Sometimes an unanticipated gust of darkness
Abruptly stops the mellifluous music of life ...
The scenery of the silver screen,
Do the effusive and emotional poets ever get contented
In searching the glistening moonbeams in endless darkness
And in counting scintillating stars from the lawn!

Every darkness doesn't bring a moonlit night!
Even a flower can't fill itself with colours in the dark,
How the colours of life can be radiant then?

Yet, it is time to hold a fistful of fireflies
To gather some light and lustre.
We have to search for the harmonious note
from the clinking and blinking sounds of the broken glasses
now, the wait is only of a few moments
For a resplendent shining morning to knock.

●

The Vanquished Time

Does time really make us forget everything?
Now, a question on time has come to my mind!

I still remember, as if it happened yesterday
The childhood days...
Swinging on the prop roots of a banyan tree,
playing up and down on a bullock cart
swimming across the rising river
dipping down the head in the water to catch a fish
and playing the game of stealing the bride in the riverside!

The time could not make me forget
The nuances of childhood festivities.
Not forgotten fasting, worshipping,
Offering for good fortunes.
Traditional jubilation of Festivals
Of summer, spring and harvest months,
the folk songs, music, dance are never forgotten.
Neither the lamentation nor moaning of
Crazy homeless Kanchan in hunger
nor the moments spent sleeping on the roof top
While trying to recognize
The Great Bear and the Pole Star are forgotten!!

It is still fresh in my mind the crooked roads to school,
The aluminium box and the colourful stickers on it,

Friends and quarrels with them,
broken and fixed friendship again,
many classmates and especially the girl
Who always was crying even in minutest issue…
Are still fresh in my mind!!

The time has failed to erase the memories of
My beloved's teary eyes looking at me
while sitting in the wedding stage....
The unseen anguish of pain given
By someone very close and bosom,
the helpless look of my dear mother
While I shifted to town leaving my village behind,
the pitter-patter of papa's sandals while
Walking along me to see me off at my village bus stand,
And a few words of reassurance...
"Study hard, do not worry about us..."
Can never be erased from my memory.

Who says!
Time can change anything...
May it be big or any small incident, we forget everything,
the past gets lost in the oblivion,
and never comes back again!!

●

The Cascading River

It is impossible for the river
To flow without two banks!

The river keeps herself confined
within the boundary of both the ends.
It never surmounts the banks.
It ties itself with abstinence and reverence,
in controlled attachment with disciplinary decorum.
And when it surpasses the banks ...
It can bring along loads of sorrows
the river may be horrendous like a swelling sea!!

It envelopes everything as if it is the empress
Of all affection, love, grandeur and wealth ...
Buckles up and flows with discipline
To dispense and distribute
Bliss, good fortune and life!
Neither has it needed anyone's support
Nor any permission and acclamation, requires no praise!!

The river flows all alone ahead.
No babbling and gurgling are heard.
Neither sighs nor the boatman's chantey sail on air!
It endures the process of relentless flow,
even in the crowd of both banks
The river remains unconnected and solitudinous ever!

The river can be a benign beauty
it can be like goddess Annapurna or Saraswati.
Offers Shalligrams to worship,
Creates the divine sounds of Omkar
And hymns of Gayatri with cosmogonic vibrations.
The whole life it witnesses the reality of brazier to pyre.
It smiles and weeps surreptitiously,
Wipes out the tears, gets gloomy and melancholic,
Yet it flows on its way incessantly!!

The river can be friendly and intimate.
At times it can cause catastrophe too.
It can give life and also can take it away.
It can contain and maintain the earth
and cause dissolution as well.
It takes birth and gets extinct and disappears.
It appears to be wholesome, brings glory to both the lineage
Alike a benevolent daughter!!!

●

The Light House

The lighthouse stands still and tall.
It stands bold, stoic and indifferent,
and works with perennial persistence as well.

Since the day it stood upright,
it hasn't lowered itself yet.
It has never waited for any praise,
Never becomes disturbed by any criticism.
Whether there is any prominence of its presence
it has never bothered for,
it still stands bold, stoic and indifferent.

It restricted many a time
Signalled with different means.
It always alerted before time and any untoward happening
without any expectation in return.
It has set its own limitations and boundary
it still stands bold, stoic and indifferent.

Now the light house is left abandoned
in the middle of the sea
in an unknown island.
Dealing with the blow and thrash of time waves
it has not yet uncarted even in the sun, rains and storms.

Not shaken in the bone biting freezing winter chokes
not broken with the daily tidal strokes.
It still stands bold, stoic and indifferent.

The lighthouse doesn't flow in water
nor floats in the flow.
Never gets wearied.
It can neither move an inch from its own place
Nor gets easily vanquished.

The lighthouse stands as it is ...
Bold, stoic and indifferent,
working continually and relentlessly.
Whenever I saw its shadow...
I always find myself in its entity.

●

The Incarcerated

Now he is completely a loner
Amidst this limited and narrow world.
His life is confined within the four walls of parochialism
The geography beyond the skylight is an outer space for him.

He washes the stains of past with tears.
He draws with the cinders
All over the whole wall
rivers, mountain, trees....
There are no sky and birds in his drawings.
And no sunrise there too.
But, there a lightless solitudinous sunset does exist.

Whether the amount is more or less,
he never bothered about and doles out
the folio of darkness between the night and the day.
For him there was no difference between the night and the day.
Why would he differentiate?

He awakes neither by the sentry's whistle
nor with any roaring sound.
The idols of his temple are lost
in the inexhaustible plentiful moss.
For whom will he be conscious?

The waves of loneliness were ridging in the storm of tears
The stones were decaying with salt,
But only the lips can spell out
how much blood soaked by it.

He is that lost person whom no one ever looks for.
He is imprisoned ... in the cage of hope in uncertainty,
of consideration in possibility,
of attribution in ascension,
of conceit in existence ...
And incarcerated within own self.

No More Tears

He is prohibited to shed tears.
How can he shed tears?
Who has given that right to him!!
He doesn't have that right
No, he can't shed tears...
No, never ever he can.

Who doesn't get pain!
Who doesn't suffer now and then!!
Something or the other breaks here
Something or the other gets lost ...
Though he lost something and something got broken even
And if rarely he becomes prey to any unsaid misfortune ...
Yet, will he shed tears just because of this!
No, he just cannot shed tears.

Doesn't anybody get burnt with the cinder of deceit?
Who hasn't experienced the mushiness in a misty deception!
The darkness of disrespect and envy spread their musical
wings alike the night.
This darkness won't last forever,
He has to stand upright like an electric pole.
He has to be on fire inch by inch
to disperse handfuls of gleaming light.
He is prohibited to sing the songs of disappointment.

He can come out of all illusory attachments someday
all the whammies can end someday.
He can stand as solid as a rock
May remain infallible, determined, persistent.
But, he just cannot shed tears.
He is restricted to shed tears,
Yes, strictly denied.
If he bewails, then how can be he counted as a man!

●

The Voidness

There is shadow of abound emptiness all around us.
Tell me what created the emptiness between us?
Do I deserve this kind of halos of emptiness?

I am breathless too in an unknown hollowness.
Perhaps, I did not deserve this suffocating lonesomeness.

Yet, where did this much of voidness afloat between us?
Perhaps I do not have the answer to this.
Do you want to search for its answer?

If you know, then deliver.
No, I do not have the answer either.
But, won't it be fine if we search for the answer together?

I wonder, how can we together search for?
Now, we are standing quite a distance afar.

Leaving your hands, I haven't gone anywhere.
I still stand with you firmly as before,
In one of those valleys where the solitudinous infinite waves resonate
And the heart feels the fit of pang intensely.

I couldn't even step up my feet further.
I am still there where I was earlier.

Now unable to see anything ahead,
for the deep dense mist around me....
Impenetrable mist is everywhere.

When it becomes smoky all around
We can't see what happens in between,
It feels scary though,
You could spread your hands and see how secured it feels,
When I hold them with deep conviction.

Unbearable instability have cropped up deep inside me.
Now, don't know whether my compassionate call could
Reach you crossing the bleak void of the sea.

Do you think, you will succeed to restrict yourself?
Then cross the line you have drawn for yourself.

The voidness is nothing but an illusion ... a chimera!
Perhaps it is only a zephyr of love and resonance
Rather than a thick veneer of sullenness.

●

In Search of Truth

The man, who considers
Smile, tear, love, separation, life, sufferings,
are nothing but a bunch of lies,
is waiting for the only truth ...death!

How would he know!!
To cover the earthly body,
He would need the red silk sheet of his choice,
Which he wanted life long, will be sought for.
And tears will flow from the eyes smiled with him ever!!

Without anyone's knowledge,
someone may offer a handful dried rose petals near the feet,
stored in the velvety cloth since many years!!

They will cook all the items he likes and serve in the leaf cup
For someday relatives may experience
the bereavement of death rituals.

The incomplete desire for boating in the Ganges
will also be fulfilled,
when the remaining bones and embers
will be immersed in the Ganga.
To find out the truth, do not know how many lies
will be sacrificed!!

Death is the only eternal truth.
But, does one know...
death belongs to none.
Death comes and goes on its own terms.
It does care neither for anyone's expectations nor disregards.

●

Yes, I Am Alive!

How are you?
Hmm, am alive!!
Hey! we all are alive!

As we are alive,
we are tied with some or the other attachments,
we greet for good moments.
Sometimes you look for me and I look for you.
If we weren't alive, how would we look after each other?
We seldom look for a dead creature?

As we are alive,
We are roaming after the delusive bodiless existences,
in this revolving and whirling earth.
We are wallowing and revelling in mire and bemoaning grief.
In the forbidden areas of heart,
the sighs of weariness shout intermittently.
We are afflicted and poppling with greed, wrath, and anguish.
We are wet in tears like the dew enamelled beatific night jasmines.

As we are alive,
there are daily happenings and asks,
Such as dawn and dusk
Brightness and darkness
All kinds of dramas, acting and many different characters,
Sustenance and struggle

War drum, triumphant trumpet of conquest
Victory defeat...
Death is the last bell of the final defeat.

As we are alive,
all our desires are ochre coloured alike the tender sunrays
They get afresh with each new dawn,
Get ready to fly again,
Everyday build a large edifice of their new imagination...
Search for the lost answers to the riddles one by one.

As we are alive,
we treat treachery with loyalty,
Create rivers and oceans of frenzied insularity.
The farina and pollens of intolerance have
tuned the whole sky deep dark...
Innumerable pages of our history are filled with
blood and tears,
thirst and mirage,
trust and betrayal.

Who checks colour and looks after our decease?
Everything gets faded with the aroma of tuberose blossomed
near the heap of ashes.

●

A Loser

After gathering beaming moonshine the whole night,
I searched a lot for a white canvas
to fill colours of my dreams.
By the time I found the canvas, the brush was lost,
And the drawing board was broken.
All the beaming colours on the palette were dried up too.

Imbued all the capital I accumulated ...
a little earth, a little sky, some trust, some imagination
a little cloud, wind, and radiance
a little red, blue, green.
I had imagined to compose an unquestionable world ...
But a directionless star from an unknown galaxy
Destroyed my imaginary space!

In the twilight hours of the dusk
the red bud I drew that day
upon the bed of seashore
has blossomed today.
But do I able to cherish or worship it!
The desire for blooming flower is nothing but redolence
And this deep aromatic attachment is gradually fading.

There is no trampling of going back,
As you departed silently with the passionate restless wind.
Till day I savoured your talkative and beauteous eyes in mine.

I will be waiting as tranquil as a stone slab on the river bank
till you come back with your coloured feet.

After losing everything
Besides, the "I" what else remains?
Like a lost soldier
I can get unarmed
I can surrender
can imprison myself in your prison of love,
till the epoch time.

The Parched

People are squirming in the middle of the Sea
To get a pail of fresh water...
There are fathomless water all around.
But where is that drop of water
enough to quench the thirst??

In the middle of the deep ocean,
He was searching for a drop of potable water.
Alike me looking for an authentic human being
amidst the ocean of people.
Everyone is poignant and busy like the waves,
occupied in their own way of life.
None has time for another
Nothing worries anyone!!
Even if one stabs someone in the middle of the road
Or anyone meets an accident and writhing badly...

From dawn to dusk many known faces,
Varieties of greetings,
Numerous smiles, affection and reception,
Invitation, welcome, and hearty sermon;
These needless gratuitous affection
are not less salty than the sea water.
To build and cherish a selfless relationship...
for little affinity and congeniality,
The mind feels on the edge and becomes restive.

The Lass from Different Agnate

Your advent to my life is
like the golden ray of morning Sun.
With your arrival,
the paths of my life has got illuminated,
And now my identity is a complete one.
Like a flower, you filled my life with loads of fragrance.
Your half lisped tender sermons has turned
my unruly scattered life
to a life of harmony and exuberance.

Every single little kernel are amassed
to create a pearl mansion for you,
I was decking up the dreams for your
golden future with the colours and glue.
I am just like your mirror image,
You are the smile on my lips.
Whenever my lips sip the drops of tear
You get dull and gloomy with the slightest view.

One day you will turn into another agnate.
Though I knew it righteously,
Yet I cannot comprehend this really.
There are immense untold pain in my heart
and even time has not forgotten those reckoning ...
that one day I too made someone as another agnate.
Perhaps, time is taking revenge for that.

The Sea

A lot of sand castles are made and broken in the sea shore.
The fantasy to make a world of own flows like a river.
Some are busy in searching for livelihood,
While some others are gathered here in search of tranquillity
away from hustle bustle of life,
forgetting the livelihood for some moment.

The scrawny raw-boned beach vendor
searches life in the spicy puffed rice.
Arranging the bamboo basket...
As if he is blessing his child,
calculating the coins whether it would be enough for
the tuition fee of his child, medicines of his old mother.
And his wife's saree is yet the last item to be purchased.
What about his daughter's marriage?
These all are nothing but the wishes of Lord.
He only knows what He has thought for.

The hawker is gathering soft petal like dreams
by selling teeny and weensy things,
where handfuls of happiness
come floating with the smoke of a cup of tea.
Colourful balloons keep afloat
with the touch of bracing breeze.
The mind unwinds and unfurls waves of happiness
and the maiden's heart gets stolen.

Oh! people cramming the sea shore,
who desire to dump all the sorrows deep in the ocean.
Remember! She is the mother of worthy gems,
Poured bliss and joy profusely.
Her waves always danced in rapture with you rhythmically.
By wiping your eyes
she became too salty.
She never kept anything with her.
Rather gave away and offered you bounteously.

After Losing Something

On the way back from the market,
Yester evening I lost somewhere my wallet.
Inside it there were some money,
A list of certain important things,
One or two unpaid bills...
My driving licence and the ATM card went missing
Still it doesn't matter.
But it was very painful
as I lost, along with the wallet, your last letter.

Ohh! So troublesome it was when I lost my mobile,
The contact details, addresses, passwords...
everything was lost with that handset.
I couldn't even book a cab,
couldn't inform anyone that I lost my phone.
Suddenly, I felt as if I am a missing person.
Of course, bought a new mobile soon after.
All applications were installed as before.
Now everything is much faster and clearer.
Yet, the dearth of something bothers...
I still recall and cherish that selfie
We took from the sanctuary's watch tower.

Nothing new if something is lost.
Some or the other person certainly finds it.
But, what if once lost...
the deep heartfelt lifetime love,
the lucid dreams one visualizes whole nights,
the faith that blooms like the spring...
and moreover, if the remaining essence of humanity is lost !!

●

An Illusory Deer

If she wouldn't have been rigid that day
to get the gilded golden deer for her!!

To nurture a golden deer was not so essential.
Even it was not so easy to catch hold of it
Yet, it was just an illusory deer after all!!

Illusory deer always roam and loiter around.
Intricately they interlace the web with their aromatic musk.
Even they can afire the house of lacquer with the fire of the brume,
Where a prudent can also get misguided too
and keeps chasing the golden deer.

The illusory mirage
the sky, the Aether
the nether world
Water, earth, fire, air
from east to west
here, there and everywhere
there is the vociferous roar of temptation.
The chase has not stopped ever
even after a fatigue, a weary and gory conclusion.

The illusory gilded deer are very fallacious.
Everywhere exists the loud repetitive neigh of "save me Laxman".
But in vein...
Now one has to draw
the imaginary lines of Laxman for self-discipline.

●

The Bond

The desire to be away and unfastened from every bond,
Attachment, fondness and association is also a bond.
Liberation is alike a mirage
and metamorphosis of connection.

Attachment for denial,
Proclivity to stay attached in detachment…
everything is all about the illusion of verity and falsity.
It is a delusion to hang on to a void entity.

The moon looks beautiful from the earth
and the earth from the moon.
As the flower blossoms in obscure places
has more elegance and charm.

In the state of perplexity of
unconsciousness and consciousness,
the unsystematic indifferent heart
has a cupidity for a plethora of bonds.
Along with, an ordinary human has
an endless fascination for emancipation.

Winsomeness

Do not know why
it always feels scary in darkness.
But it always feels delightful in moonlit night!!

Do not know why
the blue colour,
mellow poetic sounds of flute,
tender love bites,
dew drops,
falling night jasmine,
the pleasant temptation for petrichor,
painted butterflies,
snowy mountains
and valley of flowers …
are highly enchanting!!

Do not know why
I love
to look at you endlessly and intently,
when you gaze at me silently.
But I feel as if this silence is the lull before the storm!!

In spite of all these,
do not know why
it feels charming to see hair locks on your face
and the small strip of smile on your lips !!

Question Mark

Is light mandatory to see things around?
Does everything look clear in bright day light?
Is it true if one has eyes, can see everything?
But what about the things we see with eyes closed?

Do only the roads, yards, roofs get wet when it rains?
The eyes often get moist sans any rain!
The heart starts sobbing!
Do clouds are the only reasons for darkness?
Or other factors are liable too?

When there is flood,
does the river only pass over and break the bank ?
Is there any limit to its devastations?
Don't anything else float in flood water
along with roofs, trees, heaps of haystacks ?

The tear soaked eyes,
the heavy and sulked hearts,
The fading and maundering dreams,
Benumbed pitiful songs of hunger,
Resonant Hamsadhwani raaga of love,
Madhuvanti raaga of deceit,
Is there any letter left to read?
Question arises repeatedly
is everyone unlettered here?

Flower of Cactus

Whensoever I chose to trade on in a crossroad
I was being hopeful like a river to merge in the Ocean.
Do not know why,
each time I got lost in an abandoned lake
or in an extensive desert.

Whensoever I sought for a little water in thirst,
Either I got a vessel full of blood
or an urn filled with tears.
When the crocodile dragged me
from the bank till middle of river,
I couldn't even say
that I have left the liver inside the tree hole.

The pervasive wings of clouds have cladded
all the rainbows designed and drawn.
My lullabies lost their splendour and radiance
with the vibrations of the kettle-drum.
I have laid numerous nets all around my garden
To catch the flamboyant butterflies.
Now the time has come to apply perfumes to bougainvillea
And sell them exorbitantly.

Till the time,
Neither I could learn how to bloom lily in tears
Nor to grow cactus in blood.

When you Left!!

After you left off,
On my way while returning today,
it was lashing down throughout.
It was good that I was drenched.
Otherwise, what would I tell why I was wet?

After you left off,
all the cherished desires had been effaced.
The glinting fire of the tiny stars
in the indifferent but undefiled sky
gradually were fading out.
Sans you the season of my helplessness
was stretching and unfolding its form inside me,
And the thatched roof of my dreams was burning.

Do you know?
While returning,
a dove nest had fallen down from a tree on the road.
The yolk and the peel of the fresh egg
had broken and spread all over.
With the loud call of rain,
the marble tomb of her dreams had smashed and shattered;
where I could very well see my reflection.

After you left off,
the earth gets moist every time when it rains,
Yet, I could not get the enchanting aroma
of petrichor anymore.
The tassels of memories fall like the night queen,
Still, I could not see your footprints in the sodden earth.

●

Illusion

Does every question has an answer to it?
Even you do not seek one,
yet fall many unsolved questions
like the leaves fall in Spring.
Why do you sound so rigid for an answer of every question.
Hmm, I afraid how will you capitulate so easily?

Anyone's absence can never stop anything in this world.
Are we really helpless sans each other?
Time teaches us the ways to live life without a lot of things.

Ragged and starveling are Gods, roaming on the roads.
Exhausted after making heavens for every other person.
They dwell under trees or by the roadside.
The wick gets burnt and the lamp gets doused.
But the baskets full of fruits,
Pails of milk are offered for the accession of a black marble.
The magnificently spectacular temples we make,
Does God really reside in it?

It is always erring and delusive.
All is illusion of wisdom,
misconception of dominance,
illusion of civilization, gentility,
delusion of truthfulness,
delusion of godliness,
Above all the illusion of finding the God.

Gambling

Life is a game of the dice.
Sometimes I lose and the other time you lose.
But one has to lose any way.

I can lose everything even for a drop for your love.
As if love is Shakuni' s dice,
And you win the game all the time.
Whereas I surrender myself again and again.

Life is a long road with
four way intersections alike the dice board.
The flame in the middle attracts you to play the game.
Whether you win or not,
yet it clearly implies that
you have to aflame yourself if you want to proceed.

Life is nothing but a game of dice.
I lost everything to win you.
But alas !
At last I lost you too.

●

Existence

Since you are there
For which everything has perpetual permanence.
There exist love, forgiveness and attachment for Nirvana.
Otherwise, everything is indiscernible.

Since you are there
the weary and exhausted eyes
fill with the hope of another shining dawn.
You are the reason for which
I seek the resonance of
your presence in every melodious tone.
The fascination for life unfolds and unrolls
Since you are there.

Since you are there,
I fall for the azure colour,
Love the gentle fragrance of blue geranium,
the rhythmic beating of the mridangam,
tender devotional hymns,
and the agreeable dedications.

I do exist as you are there
your existence makes my presence prominent,
Without you I am indigent,
Everything appears to be
disharmonious and ineptly incoherent.

Paper Boat

Childhood days were awesomely different
Completely peerless.
The innocence of tearing
The math copy for making
Tiny paper boats,
And letting those sail in the rain water
Were unmatchable and distinct.

These days it doesn't require to wish for rain.
For each night is a showery night.
I tear pages of promises
From the diary of the memory lane
To make paper boats
And sail in the flow of tears,
in the ridges of anguish.

In the deep dark solitude
Now a days, it feels easy
To pen down the analytics of life,
The limitations of meeting,
The theorems of separation,
Are alike the lines of mathematical equations
Used to be written on the classroom blackboard.

The childhood days were disparate.
The subject on the blackboard would
Change with the scheduled time table.
There is only one equation of getting and losing.
It is neither about science nor grammar now.
The calculations of life can never be wiped out.
However despite repeated efforts.

●

Forgetfulness

Whether you remember or not
Perhaps you forgot.

Usually we forget many happenings.
Things get erased from our mind.
As 'Me' too one of such issues,
Which could be forgotten easily.
There is nothing unusual to forget me.

Tell me!
Is it good to forget?
Or it is not so good?
Should we or shouldn't?
But, can everything be remembered till the end?
We lose out memories of some happenings
Just like we lose if an object is broken.

Do not know how people forget happenings so easily?
It pains severely
if someone very close to forgets you.
Surely, the mind gets disturbed …
Sometimes it is painful to pass over certain incidents.
Yet, we feel light and relaxed
when we deliberately forget certain issues.

Forgetfulness is like an ocean.
And in the heart of the ocean
plenteous thoughts are submerged.
What comes back with the ridges of wave
Those only are memories.
Some are virtues, some are sins.

●

Beyond Expectations

I wished for a little darkness
And a fistful of scalding fire
To complete the obsequies of
the awful eerie components
Of the sins that I committed never!
Around me, I feel an endless
Deep dense darkness
And outlandish fiery flame,
While searching clues for my innocence,
Sometimes I lost myself
In dingy sombre,
Other time seethed in sluggish flame.

I beseeched a fistful of silence
A quiet sea
To listen to a grasshopper's
Chirrup and cracklings,
the mumble chuckle
of the robin,
And to make a whole sandcastle.
The whole ambit is ruled by
The loud clamour of tranquillity.

Am frightened of my own
Rumbling and echoing breath
Even the warbling and

Chirping of birds
Sound like the broken
Strings of a chordophone
Seems to be quivering and pulsating,
Imbued with poignancy.

Now am a confused
Vagrant bird of a new moon night
Unsure of the morning twilight and the dawn
Yet have to return to the nest.

The Touch

The first touch,
The kick from mother's womb,
Belief,
Innocence,
Tender love,
Immaculacy,
Purity,
Virtuousness,
Are the ceaseless hymns of motherly love !

Your touch,
The ripples of frisson,
Quivering,
Inner secrecy,
The soul,
Cognizance,
Credence,
Impetuosity,
Fondness,
Devotement,
Admission,
Hope,
Solace,
Are love's passionate uninhibited longings!

Indecorous touch,

Immorality,
Trickery,
Brutality,
Affliction,
Ailment,
Bewailing,
Sin,
Scars of aspersion
All are nothing but
Iffy shudderings!

Touch resonates affection
Touch reverberates love
Touch creates utter dismay
Touch starts with the mother
And dissolutes on the mother earth.

The River

After getting you
I plunged deep into the Chandrabhaga like Dharama.
As if my hands are chopped off
alike the genius artisans of the Tajmahal.
You are my architect
You are my only edifice.
I do not have any ardent desire to build
another Konark or a Tajmahal either.

I am only impassioned that
you keep burbling and rippling
And flow like the curly and wavy
Chandrabhaga or Yamuna.
I remain inundated incessantly
with your devastating overflow.
I will be playing flute on the shore
like an innocent herdsman,
Or else I may wallow down like an Aghori
By smearing the ash from a half burnt corpse.

Sans you
neither the flute whistles
Nor the pyre of the Aghori glows.

Earth to Sky

This benevolent earth is my world
And the heavenly sky is yours.

Am unaware of
What you strove and sought for in your ecosphere,
But in my world,
whenever I experienced the reverberation of your actuality,
I feel the beautiful Spring all around my yard
And the flowers of love blossom in plenty.

The world of love is very beautiful and fascinating
Like a golden cage.
While inside the cage
A lot of affection and love being showered.
In spite of all these adoration
The bird sometimes ruffles and flutters its wings
To be lost in the azure.
But, when the cage kept open
The bird becomes dubious,
Then it seeks both the open sky
As well as being inside the cage.
Ahh! the poor helpless bird !
Cannot even decide whether to hurry off
Or to be held back as before!

It is very easy to wave bye-bye and
Bid a farewell to move from
One city to the other.
But is it that smooth to bid adieu
To the heart?
How far is the sky from the earth?
Though it is within the reach
Just at a stone's throw,
But arduous to march on to the azure!!

●

Holi

Now a days holi
is a stereotypical day of grizzly and dusty colours only.
After smearing different veneers of colours in life
Can the abeer coat the body anymore?

When the veins and vessels are charred
with sourness of envy and jealousy
with continuous attack by the talons and beaks of nocturnal
As if bled again and again,
When the petrified humanity
the impaired mentality and the soul become senseless,
Can the abeer coat the body anymore?

When faith and faithlessness
Consolation and trepidation
are washed away with deceitful love,
After becoming Neelkanth by drinking the deluded hemlock,
Can the abeer coat the body anymore?

Nothing more nothing less
Now the greed lies
in the slightest portion of the blue skies.

Poet

It is not at all easy
to be a poet.

When the poet was not a poet
He was a contented person,
Without any hesitation
He could share his happiness and sadness
He could share life's hard facts,
the gospel truth of life.
But after becoming a poet
The grammar of his life
has got completely disarrayed.

The poet when speaks out his heart,
The world accolades more
than being empathetic and considerate,
They praise and say "the lines are awesome"
They misquote the truth as the poet's imagination,
They search for the feel and soul in impulsiveness,
They fail to appreciate the heart,
instead they praise lavishly only the words.

While the poet is intoxicated in love …
With tottering feet he never utters any note of acceptance.
When he gathers courage to say
His dear beloved, "I love you" !

People say, this man is intoxicated.
What a splendid piece of creation!
the poet is a man of deep culmination.

The poet holds onto many untold feelings.
The grief and vexation coiled up
which he never could share
And the moistness of tears
find its way under the arch of the cage.

It is not so easy to be a poet!
The heat of a deep sigh melts out
The poet who could write very easily about
the star, comet and horizon
war, fear, and deception …
But he continues to be in pursuit of words
for expressing his own feelings and heart.
It is not that easy to be a poet.

The Flower

What is the worth of a flower?
How much a florist gets for a handful of flowers?
But her dried lips get delighted with a glittering smile
like the beautiful petals.
Her eyes fill with the glowing and flowing faith.

No idea, what could be the worth of a flower!
Yet, it graces a stone replicating as the God
while adorned with devoutness.
Fills the soul with hope, blessings, lasting trust
to drink the tears as divine water with culmination.

What is the worth of a flower?
It always fascinates and attracts
someone else by surrendering itself,
Decks up the beloved's chignon till wilts out,
And wipes out all its baseless sulkiness.

How long is the life span of a flower?
It is like the Sun,
blooms in the morning and fades in the evening.
It never counts its life.
However enchants uncounted lives!!

How long a flower does live?
I am unsure now,
whether to bloom flowers in my garden or
to be a flower myself.
It is yet an unsolved question.

This is Life

Perhaps life doesn't bank upon
The fact whether someone is extant or dormant anymore.
Nothing really falls apart
Rather falls in place and edges forward
In the usual way
Leaving some exceptions
Like rain, spring and autumn.

It advances and recedes
Alike the ridge of the sea...
If we make a sandcastle
On the shore with sheer
Unyielding obstinacy,
Ultimately the wave will wash it away.
How can we then blame the tide for that?

With the age we
Grow and evolve
Sit quietly on the bank in solitude
Enjoy the solidarity
And silently count the tides coming and going aback
Now, the wait is only for a gush of tide
To annihilate the sandcastle.
Nothing remains permanent here.
Life is fleeting, ephemeral and full of impermanence.

●

Pretension

Do all the heave of sighs
have emerged only from pain?
Are there earnest entreaties in the appeal of easement?

Many a time, whenever I heard the poignant outcry
of the sighs of relief,
I run unhindered
Alike the gnawed and agitated Laxman.
But all the time
I came back deceived hence wounded;
By the disguised Maricha's illusion.

Yet, with a fresh outcry for relief,
I again cross the lines of Laxman
the soul becomes restive and perturbed
to be scarred and gory with the weapon of deception.

But, each pain never can cry for a solace.
Cannot even pray for a clemency.

Happiness

Happiness is falling
Alike the hailstones fall in an untimely rain.
Before melting down,
we need to pick those up
and fix like stars in the autumn sky.
Else, the life is nothing but
darkness and an endless night.

Cheerfulness drops down like the night jasmine,
drenched in the pearl dews of dawn.
We should pluck those up from the earth
to string together into a garland as we wish.
Otherwise, life is nothing but a bed of dull and withered flowers.

Happiness is blossoming like a lock of grass.
We should peck those up to weave a wind castle
like the nest of weaver bird.
No fear of any storm nor cold can hamper it.
Otherwise, the life is not much far from a rough barren desert.

Happiness is a delighting experience.
High above the confusion of any accessibility or inaccessibility.
Cheerfulness is tightly filled in the wax fort of the honey bee
in the form of nectar.
If we can collect it we can retain the life
Or else, life is nothing but a burning thorny jungle.

Delusion

Nothing is perpetual
Nothing at all.

Neither life nor pain
Neither desire nor libation
Neither dearth nor abundance
Neither poverty nor opulence
Nothing is permanent.

Neither dusk nor dawn
Neither arrival nor departure
Neither pleasure nor torture
Neither dejection nor consternation

Neither lordship nor servitude
Neither glorification nor vilification
Neither desired nor undesired
Neither vanquishment nor affront

Neither incredulity nor transparency
Neither perishable nor immutable
Neither subjugation nor liberation
Neither penetrable nor invincible

Neither insularity nor extensiveness
Neither fortunate nor unfortunate
Neither petrified nor powerful
Neither separated nor integral

Nothing is permanent
Nothing at all
Yet .... everything seems illusory.

Mynah Soared High

The mynah wanted to fly
for days together,
I let open the door of its cage
As it wished to fly,
it did not even look back and soar up high.

The mynah surely would fly one day,
So it flew away.
I knew, it was never mine
Yet, alike Sibi I cut ounces of flesh from my body
And weighed for her.

These days, my eyes keep searching for the mynah
amongst the flock of birds returning home,
When the dusk arrives
I stick near the door.
I did not take out her cage yet
Till day I fill her plate.
Unwittingly I utter its name
As my hope for its come back still didn't fade.
My heart quivers faster
When fluttering of wings it hears,
When someone calls oh mother !
I bethink that Mynah is nearer.

Mynah flies away, just like that.
Perhaps to flit away one day, it gets caught.
But by picking up the bits and pieces,
Can a dream glasshouse be built again
in the shattered world caused by her flapping wings?

●

Incomplete

Everything is incomplete
Yet seems complete
Within the incompleteness.

Birth and death,
Inception and dissolution
All play mere mergers in the horizon
Entangled with resonance and dissonance
With distorted geometry
And sketchy eventual inevitables
As if shortfalls are the
Only ultimate wholeness.

Let it be the impoverishment or dilettantes;
Even the invigorating never ending thirst
Everything appears partial
There is no rule fixed
That all will be carried through
Neither possible nor cardinal
As we all have witnessed
Surprisingly some miniature shrubberies
Make the scene harmonious with austerity.

Foraging and exploring
The efficacy and adequacy
Within a dearth
Make you stand prominent
With a unique approach to attain and
Accomplish the search of life.

●

Butterfly Doesn't Get Caught

Race is everywhere.
Life is a race ...
From caterpillar to pupa
Pupa to butterfly
Again butterfly to caterpillar.
From dawn to dusk
And from dusk to dawn once more.

Time runs out
Not everyone can run for long coping with time.
For that time engulfs the morning in the cocoon.

I have been chasing the butterfly
Since those days till time
It flutters its wings around me
and has been clicking and cracking to say,
Since those days, and even today
"I am yours".

I never could catch the butterfly then nor today.
I stumbled down again and besmeared with blood stain
While chasing the butterfly then
The same too I face yet again.
Many colourful and painted butterflies
Frolicked and smiled beamingly with me.
Fluttered and quivered from flower to flower,

But never got caught then.
The same I am facing today again.

Race is everywhere all the while
To catch hold of a butterfly
But is it really necessary?
Yet, there is no rest,
No interlude in moving in haste.

●

The Painted Enthrallment

Though the wall appears colourless and blank
But when I see,
The engraved image of unspoken past,
Hues of exuberance,
Painted twilight of parting pain are clearly discernible.
Even the ripple of the first touch,
The fragrance of attar soaked body,
The drops of indignant displeasure
and the lotus forest of disharmonious love …
All make their presence perceptible.

The resound of my earnest invitation to you,
And the twittering of words
that caress the gloomy sombrous mind,
That tender touch of fingers and
The deep sighs those I took thinking of you,
While standing alone on the platform
All reflect on the blank wall.

I draw my desired world
On the naked wall,
Dabbing and rubbing
Different shades from the memory.

Your image emerges like the tender leaves
Peeping from the spathe of the tree.
Your scarlet red lips are
just like the petals of a phoenix flower.
I can see the expressive eyes,
the glow and the glee of going back…
As well can hear the promises of not giving up.

●

Black Eagle Books

www.blackeaglebooks.org
info@blackeaglebooks.org

Black Eagle Books, an independent publisher, was founded as a nonprofit organization in April, 2019. It is our mission to connect and engage the Indian diaspora and the world at large with the best of works of world literature published on a collaborative platform, with special emphasis on foregrounding Contemporary Classics and New Writing.

www.ingramcontent.com/pod-product-compliance
Lightning Source LLC
Chambersburg PA
CBHW060619080526
44585CB00013B/898